A Day of
Good Deeds

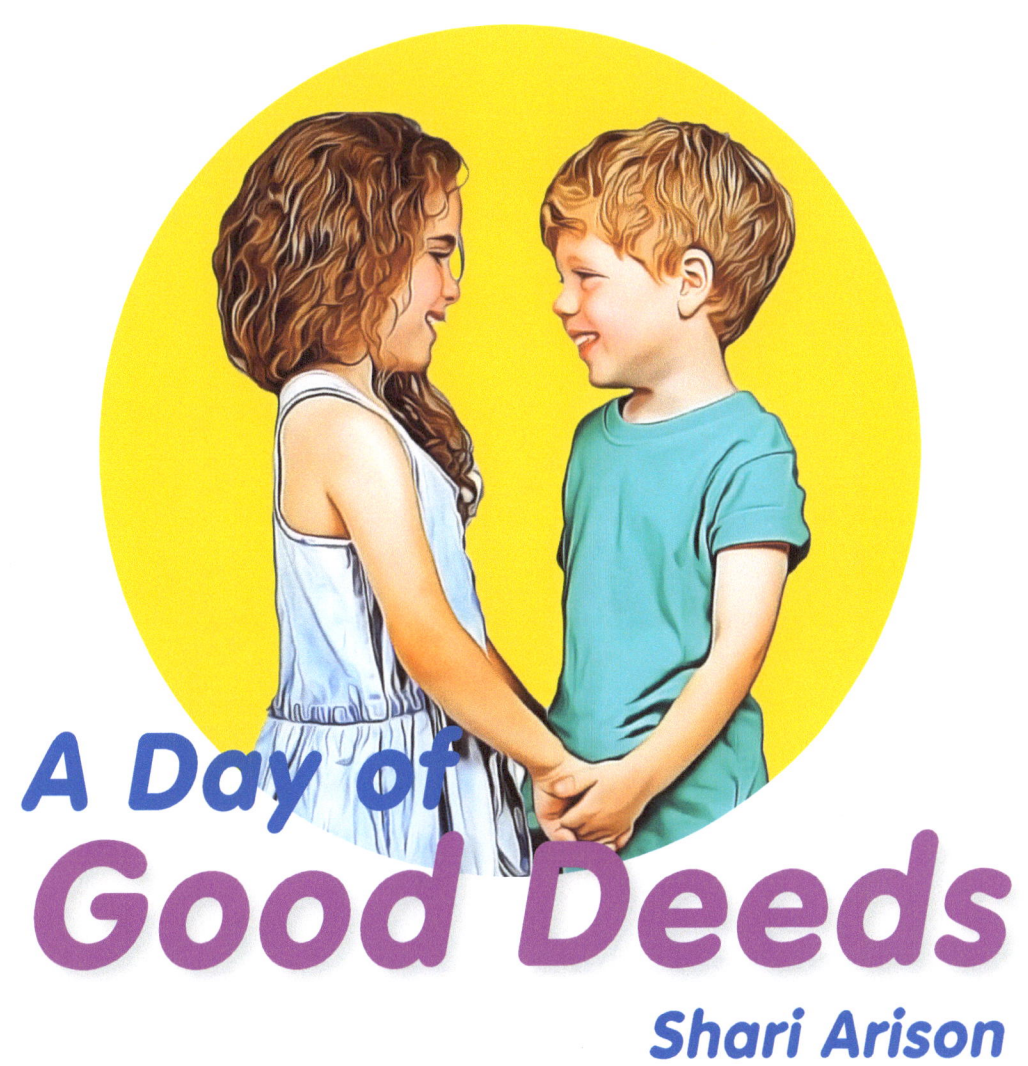

A Day of
Good Deeds

Shari Arison

Good morning, Mommy. Good morning, Daddy. I am going to think good. That way I will have a good day.

Think good
Speak good
Do good

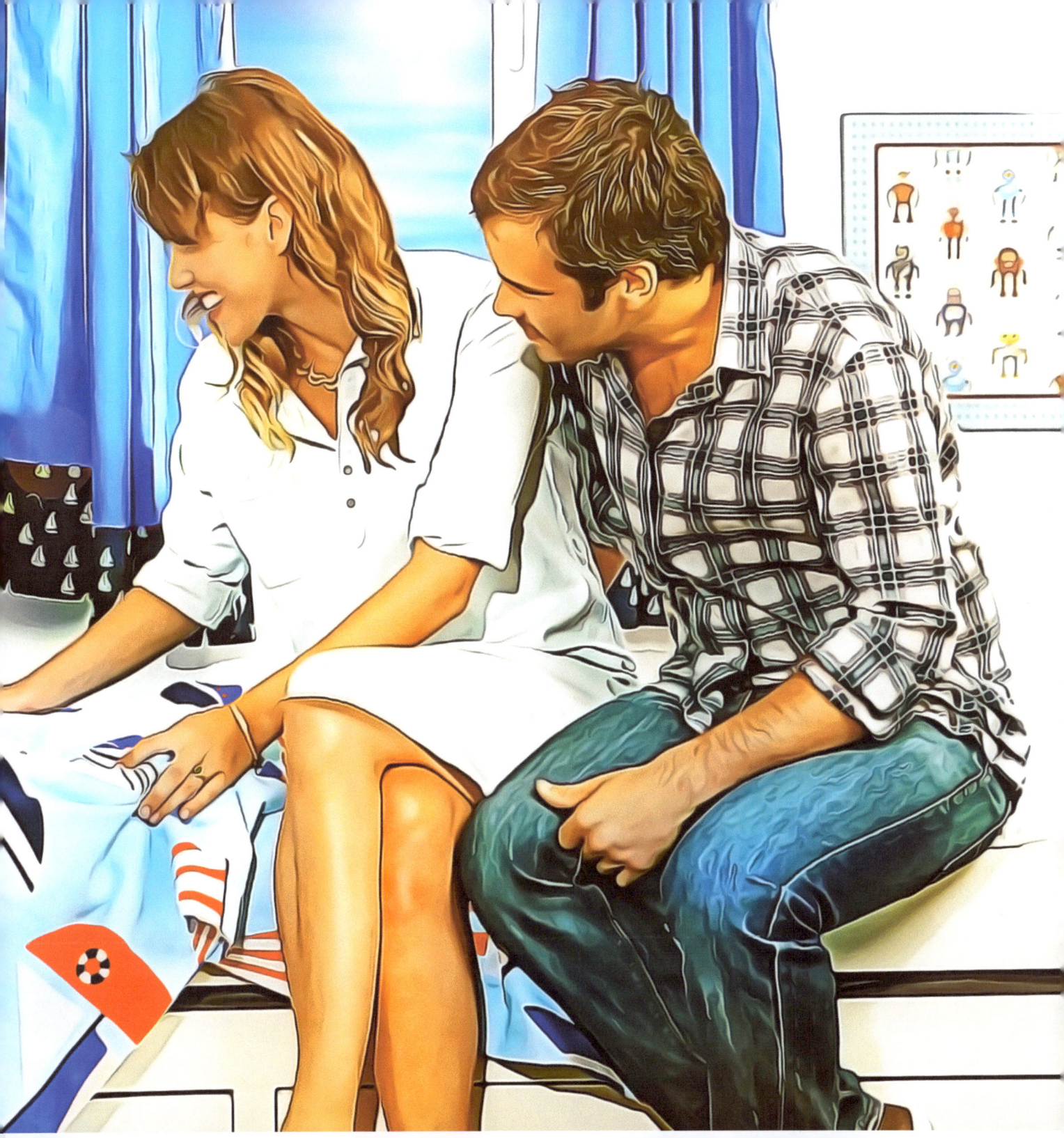

Walking in nature gives so much joy. The sky is blue, the sun is shining, and the gentle air is so soothing.

Sharing games and toys with your friends is good. Each of us plays with what we love, and we all have fun together.

Petting an animal is a lot of fun. Thank you for all creation.

Think good. Speak good. Do good.

The water purifies me, regenerates me, calms me, and makes me feel good.

It feels good to get a hug from Mom and Dad.

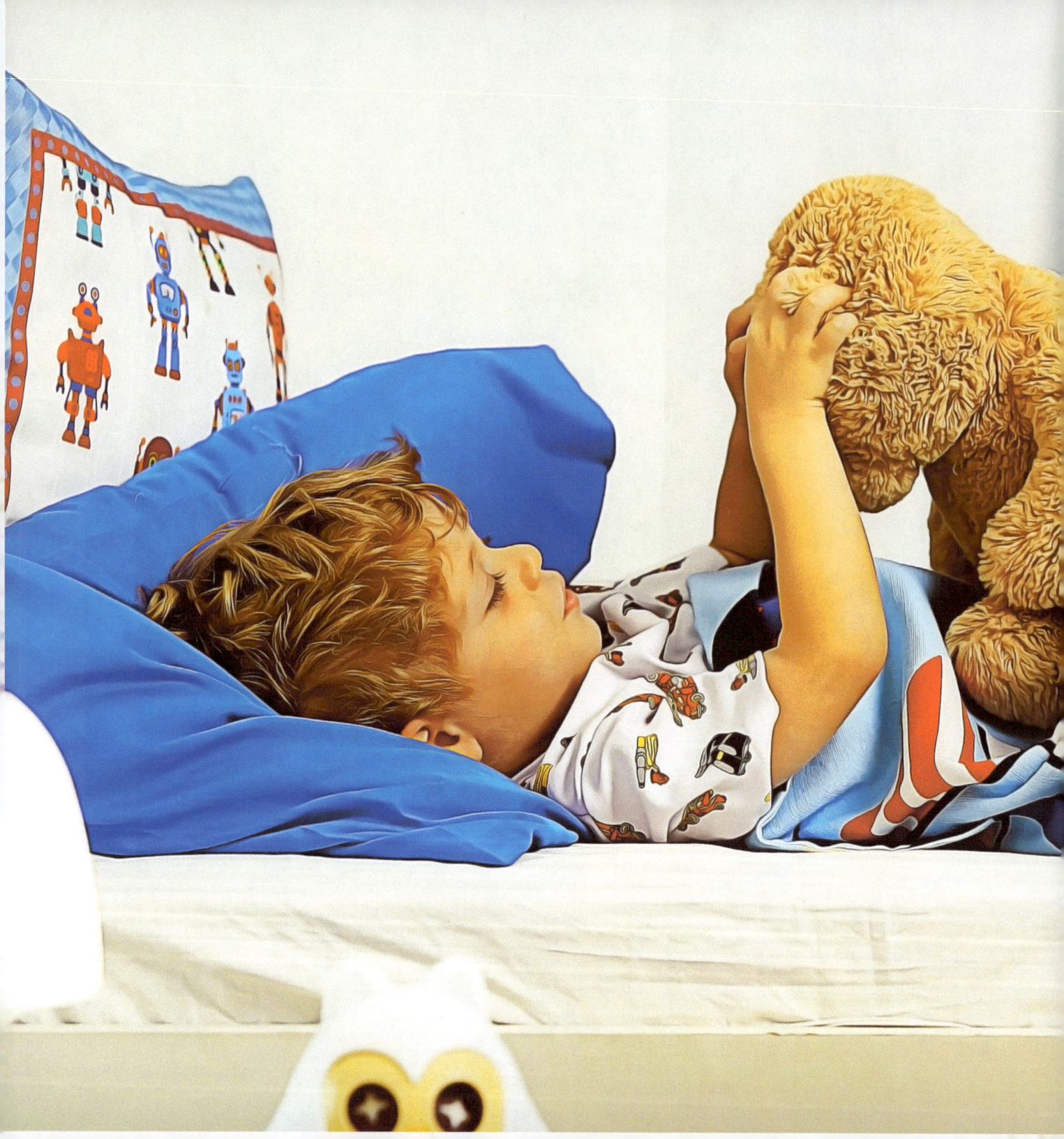

I created my day—a fun day, a good day. I will have good dreams. Tomorrow is a new day.

Think good. Speak good. Do good.

Think good
Speak good
Do good

Dedicated to all children of the light, who came to make our world a better place

Shari Arison
A Day of Good Deeds

All Rights Reserved
Text copyright © 2016 by Arison Creative Ltd.
Illustrations copyright © 2016 by Arison Creative Ltd.
English Language copyright © 2016 by Arison Creative Ltd.

Book Design: Kobi Franco Studio
Graphics : Roni Schneider
Photos: Osnat Rom
Illustration and Image Processing: Elite Avni-Sharon
Stills Production: Mialma Productions
Production: Keren Bachar Amitai
Editor of the Book: Tamar Bialik

All rights reserved. No part of this book may be reproduced by any mechanical, photographic, or electronic process, or in the form of a phonographic recording; nor may it be stored in a retrieval system, transmitted, translated or otherwise be copied for public or private use without prior written permission of the publisher.

Printed in the United States

ISBN : 978-1-937504-99-1
www.shariarison.com

www.ingramcontent.com/pod-product-compliance
Lightning Source LLC
LaVergne TN
LVHW072128070426
835512LV00003B/48